ABCMTL

JEANNE PAINCHAUD   BRUNO RICCA
TRANSLATED BY KATIA GRUBISIC

To Max and his whole new view of the city.   J. P.

To V., the woman of my life.   B. R.

LINDA LEITH
PUBLISHING

ABC
MTL

This book is a tribute to Montreal — the city I love, the city I chose when I was twenty. From A to Z, each letter shows a different aspect of Montreal. There are so many ways to explore this place, and to share it... in this case, to share it through the eyes of a child.

I discovered, or rediscovered, Montreal when my son was little. As he learned the alphabet, he started seeing letters all over the city. He pushed on, exploring further: he wanted to adopt the Biodôme's capybara (a giant hamster!), brush up against the butterflies flying free at the Insectarium, zoom down the snowy mountain, stop and listen to the musicians in the metro, kayak along the Lachine Canal, get lost in the crowd at the jazz festival, and sample the baked treats of every single culture that calls Montreal home. It's a journey through a mosaic made up of contrasts — and endless possibilities.

This book came to life with the great work of photographer Bruno Ricca, himself an adopted Montrealer for over twenty-five years, and thanks to the terrific team at Les 400 Coups. *Merci* also to Linda Leith and her team for the English edition.

Off you go: Montreal awaits!
Jeanne Painchaud

ANGEL
WINGS WIDE OPEN —

BAGEL
YES,
OURS
ARE BETTER

COLD
THE SNOWPLOW
TAKES NO PRISONERS
EVEN MY SNOWMAN SURRENDERS

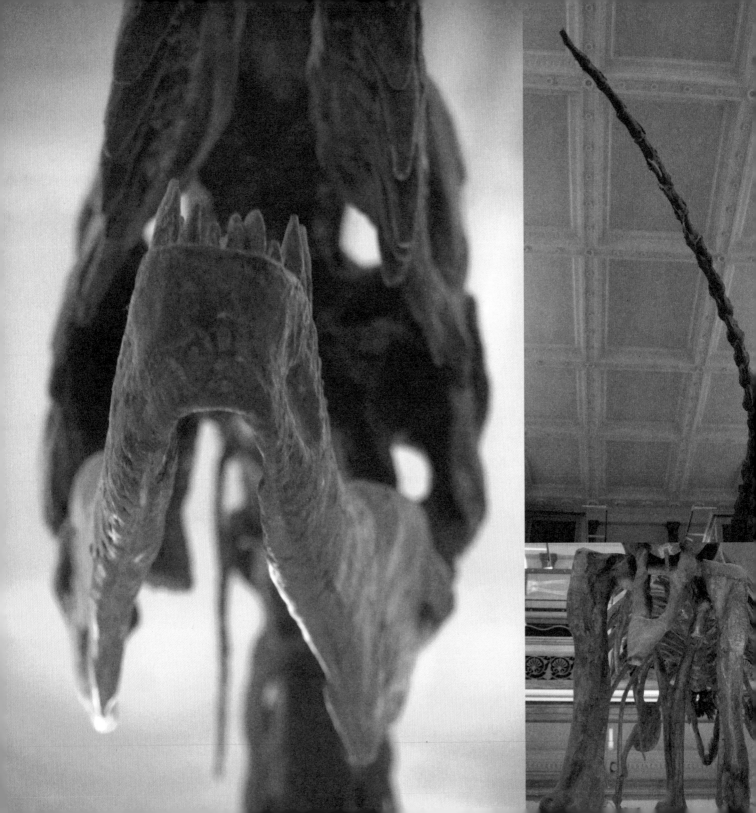

DINOSAUR
LITTLE GUY
DOESN'T LOOK
A DAY OVER 74 MILLION YEARS

EXPLOSIVE
FIRECRACKER NIGHTS
THE CITY LIGHTS UP
LIKE A BIRTHDAY CAKE

FOUNTAINS
A TRICKLE, A STREAM
RUNNING WATER
LIGHT HEART

GREEN
IN THE DOG DAYS
A FRAGRANCE OF GRASS
FRESHLY CUT

HOCKEY
THE SCRAPE, THE SPRAY, THE SLAP, THE ROAR GO HABS GO!

INSECTARIUM
CRAWLERS, STINGERS, WINGED THINGS: BUG IS BEAUTIFUL

JAZZ
DEEP IN THE CROWD
I LET IN THE RHYTHMS
OF THE WORLD

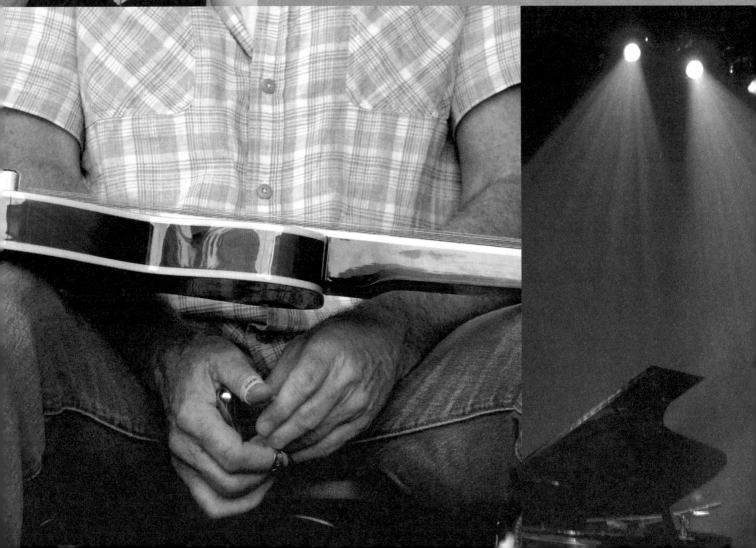

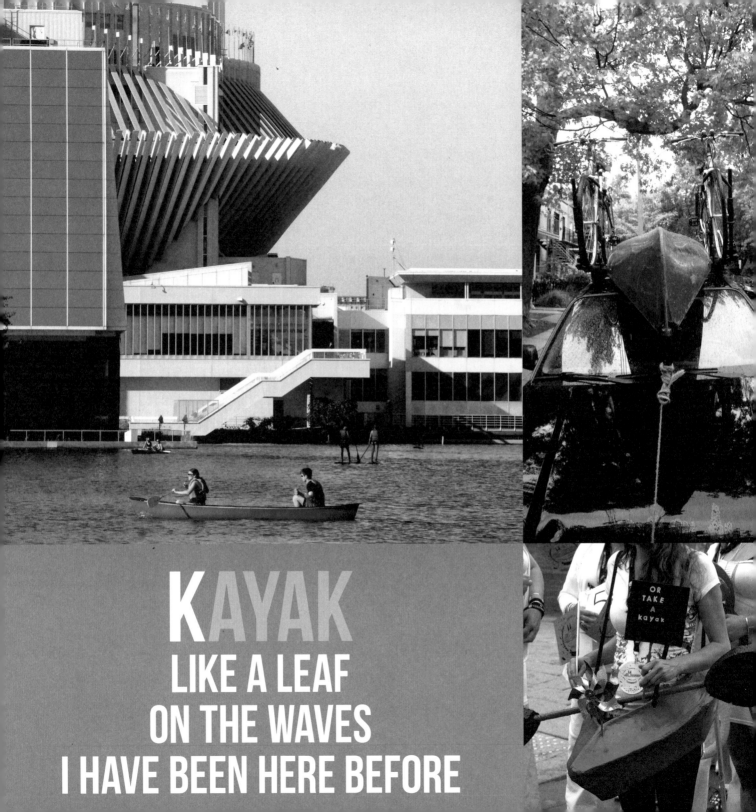

KAYAK
LIKE A LEAF
ON THE WAVES
I HAVE BEEN HERE BEFORE

LIGHT
THE BEAM
THAT SWEEPS THE SKY
A BEACON BECKONS

MOUTHWATERING

A TASTE
FOR EVERY TOOTH!

NATIONS
THIS LAND IS TIOHTIÀ:KE, HAUDENOSAUNEE TERRITORY:
SHÉ:KON, HELLO

ORANGE
BRIGHT AS THE SUN
AS FAR AS THE EYE
CAN DREAM

ZONEORANGE
C:0.0 M:48.0 Y:100.0 K:0.0

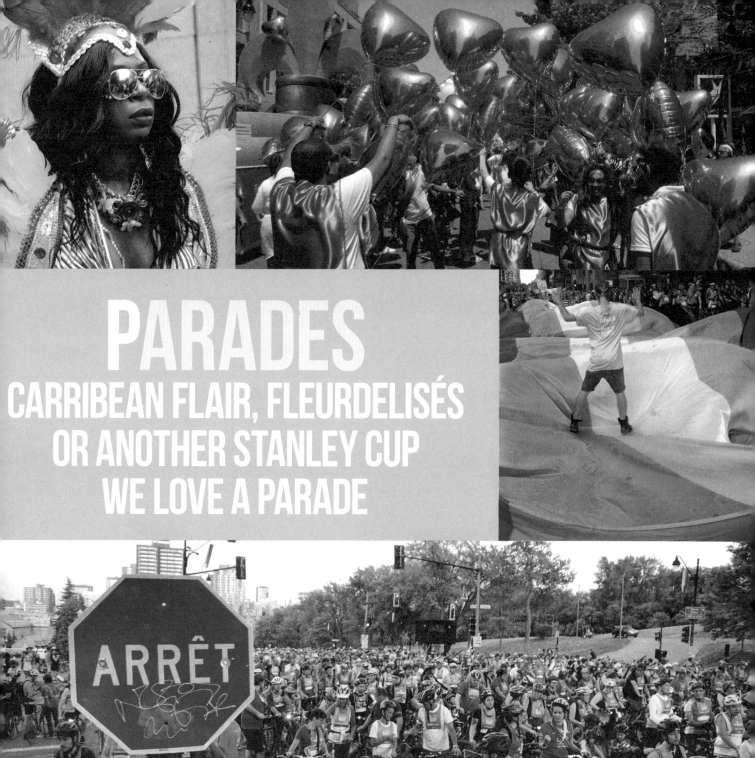

PARADES
CARRIBEAN FLAIR, FLEURDELISÉS
OR ANOTHER STANLEY CUP
WE LOVE A PARADE

QUAY
TO THE CLOCK TOWER
NEVER FASTER THAN THE CURRENT
THE PATH THAT WALKS

RAPIDS
THE RIVER BOASTS ITS OWN ROLLERCOASTER

SANDCASTLES
FOR A WINTER CITY
WE SURE KNOW
HOW TO SUMMER

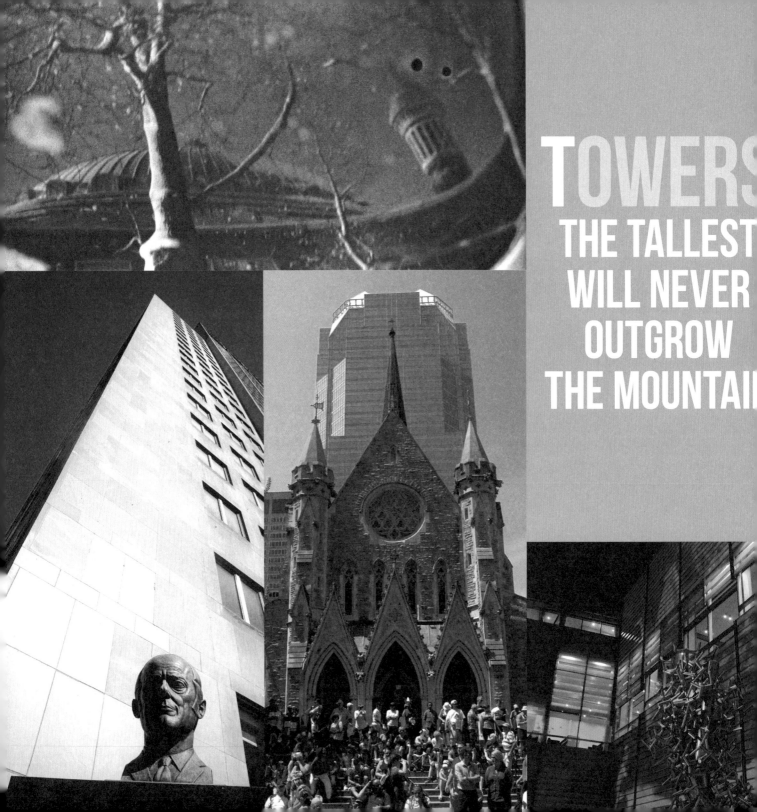

TOWERS
THE TALLEST WILL NEVER OUTGROW THE MOUNTAIN

UNIQUE
THE CHARM OF THE STAIRS IS ALSO OUR DOWNFALL SOMETIMES LITERALLY

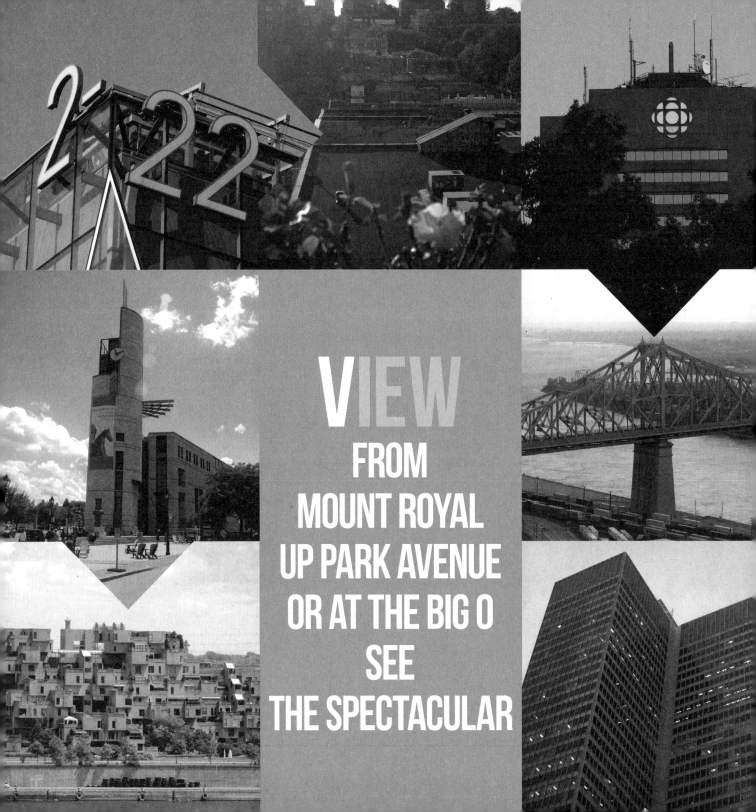

VIEW
FROM
MOUNT ROYAL
UP PARK AVENUE
OR AT THE BIG O
SEE
THE SPECTACULAR

WONDER
IN THE METRO
THE ONLY SEASON
IS MUSIC

XOX
MONTRÉAL
JE T'AIME

7 NOVEMBRE 2016 - LUNDi

SO LONG MiSTER
Léonard Cohen

IL DEMEURE CE QUE VOUS NOUS
AVEZ DONNÉ.

Élise   ARiANE
x   CLARE x
x

YAY!
ON TOP OF THE WORLD
THERE'S ROOM FOR EVERYONE

DÉFENSE DE STATIONNER

ZZZ...
AT LAST I LAY MY SLEEPY HEAD
TO ROAM THROUGH THE CITY
OF DREAMS

Eagle-eyed photographer Bruno Ricca had fun snapping the whole alphabet along St. Catherine Street, the city's longest and most fascinating commercial artery. Stretching ten kilometres from west to east, it spans the island in all its diversity, from Anglo to Franco, richer and poorer, by turns commercial, cultural, residential, and industrial, at once posh, dark, busy, deserted, jammed, decked out, festive — and always passionate. As you stroll along St. Catherine, look around: can you spot all of Bruno's letters? Or gather your own alphabet? It's up to you!

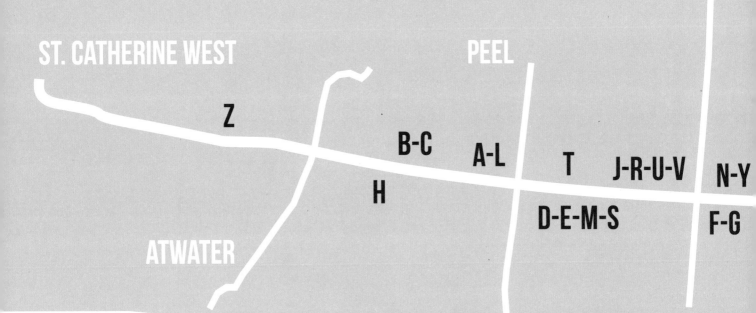

ABC**MTL**

ST. LAWRENCE
(THE MAIN)

ST. CATHERINE WEST

PEEL

Z

B-C

A-L

T

J-R-U-V

N-Y

H

D-E-M-S

F-G

ATWATER

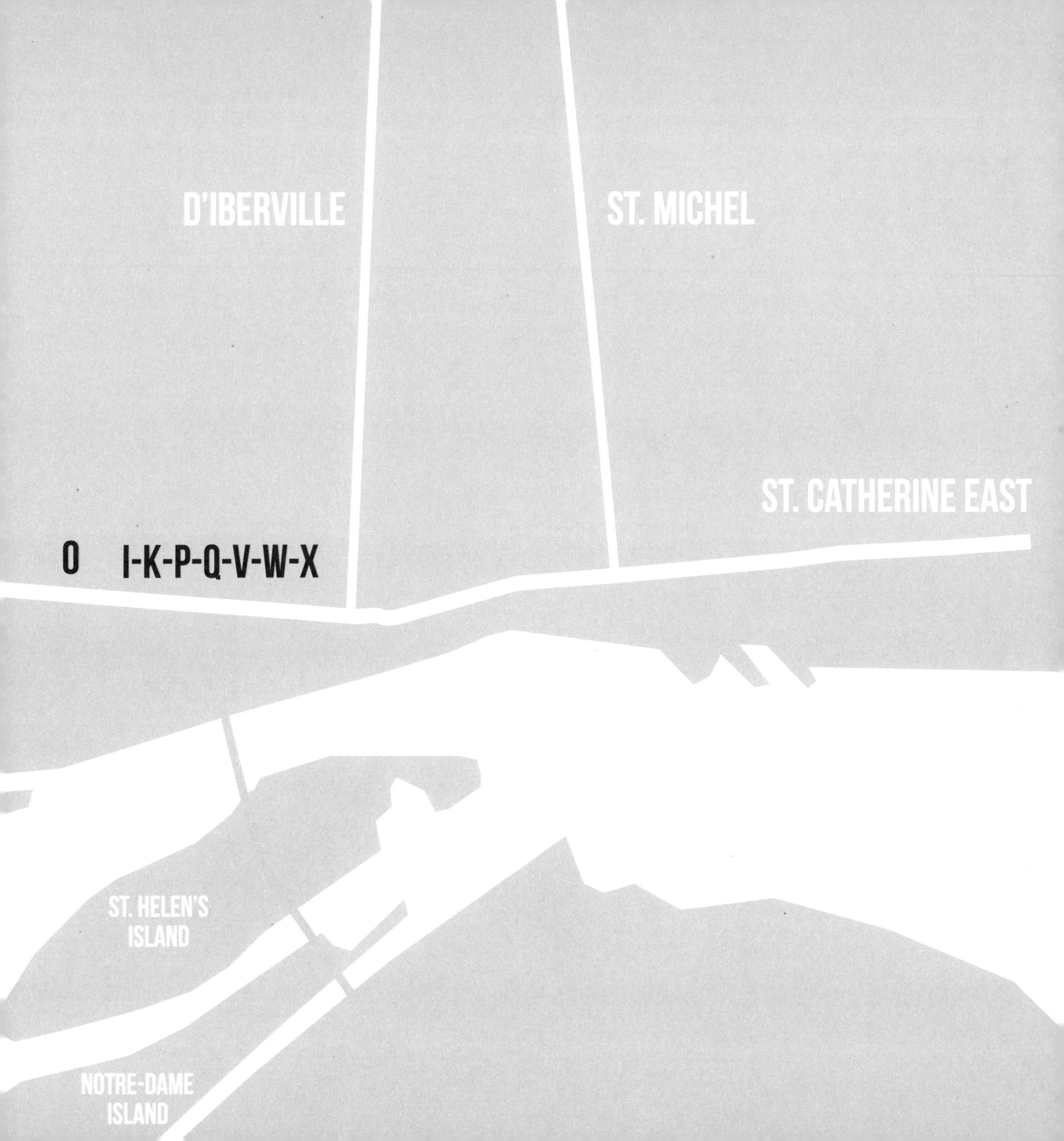

D'IBERVILLE

ST. MICHEL

ST. CATHERINE EAST

O   I-K-P-Q-V-W-X

ST. HELEN'S
ISLAND

NOTRE-DAME
ISLAND

ABCMTL

ANGEL

Perched at the top of a monument overlooking avenue du Parc, the angel stands watch over Montreal — the city known as Ville-Marie when it was founded in 1642. Since those first settlers, waves of immigrants have followed: the French and, after the Conquest of 1763, English, Scots, and Irish. Later came Jewish, Greek, Lebanese, Italian, Chinese, Portuguese, Vietnamese, Haitian, North African, and other communities. It seems impossible to identify all the distinct origins from which Montrealers have come — more than 120! Today, Montreal is the second largest French-speaking city in the world.

BAGEL

Small rings of bread, bagels are traditionally first boiled in water then baked in a wood-fired oven and rolled in sesame or poppy seeds. They are great fresh — a bite on the way home is irresistible — or toasted with cream cheese and smoked salmon. The recipe was likely brought over by Eastern-European Jewish immigrants 250 years ago. The oldest artisanal bagel factory still in operation opened in 1919 in the Mile End district. And the argument over which city, New York or Montreal, makes the best bagels has been going on at least as long.

COLD

Snow can be a child's delight, or it can be quite a headache. Montreal is known for its ferocious winters: the city is blanketed by snow from December to April, with an average of 210 centimetres falling each season. As soon as there's an accumulation of about an inch, snowplows start to criss-cross the city, packing the snow along the streets and sidewalks. Some storms, usually about four every year, dump fifteen centimetres or more... sometimes much more. Each storm sets off a complex loading operation involving hundreds of plows, snowblowers, and trucks that work to collect the snow over several days. Clearing the snow must be a favourite of the city's workers, who get a chance to be kids again.

DINOSAUR

The bones of this 74-million-year-old dinosaur were discovered in 1920 by Levi Sternberg in Dinosaur Provincial Park, Alberta, a province that has yielded many fossils of these titans from another age. The animal was a Gorgosaurus, which means "fierce lizard." This relatively small specimen would have weighed a tonne. The skeleton can be seen at the Redpath Museum, the natural history museum at McGill University. A bastion of the city's English-speaking community, McGill is the oldest university in Montreal: it was established in 1821, and named after James McGill, a Montreal businessman of Scottish origin, who had bequeathed the land where the university was built.

EXPLOSIVE

After the sun goes down over Montreal, late in the evening, the summer sky fills with bursts and with the flash of a thousand lights. Nothing to worry about; it's just the Montreal Fireworks Festival. Every summer since 1985, eight pyrotechnic firms from as many countries have tried to outdo each other. Dragging blankets and folding chairs, families huddle along prime viewing spots in nearby parks, on the banks of the river, at the La Ronde amusement park, or along the Jacques-Cartier Bridge. The show is dazzling but ephemeral, and soon the colours give way to shooting stars in the deepening dark.

FOUNTAINS

Across the city, fountains soothe Montrealers who aren't used to the heat. In the Quartier des spectacles, the Place des Festivals's surging fountains soothes and surprises the young and the young at heart with jets of water that periodically leap from the ground: a party breaks out! Down the hill, in the business district, the great painter and sculptor Jean-Paul Riopelle created *La Joute*, an astonishing fountain that breathes water, fire, and mist. At the Square St. Louis, meanwhile, benches line a statuesque Victorian fountain — the oldest in the city, built in 1880.

GREEN

When spring has finally sprung, the city begins to change its hue. Nature, which had been sleeping under the snow for months, turns green. The city starts to relax: now is the time for baseball and soccer. Friends gather for a barbecue or a picnic in one of the island's many parks. Perhaps as a vestige of the city's English ancestry, city parks have lush grass. Lawns wrap around many houses, or unfold before them, and it's not uncommon to hear the drone of a lawnmower. Perfumers visiting the city once allegedly claimed that if a scent were created in homage to Montreal, it would surely have to include notes of freshly cut grass.

HOCKEY

Montreal is a hockey city. Some kids here start out in amateur leagues, while others are die-hard street-hockey devotees or play shinny. As they get older, ice aficionados might join beer leagues, before graduating to old-timers' teams. What causes this national fever is of course the local professional team. Since the club was founded in 1909, the Montreal Canadiens have won an unrivalled twenty-four Stanley Cups, the National Hockey League's highest award. It's not uncommon to hear the rallying cry "Go Habs Go!" — the Canadiens' nickname, "les Habitants," is a reference to early French settlers.

INSECTARIUM

It was the immense collection of insects of Georges Brossard, a passionate entomologist, that led to the creation of this strange and unusual in 1990. A popular favourite with children, the Insectarium is located on the grounds of the Montreal Botanical Garden, and is part of the Space for Life natural science museum complex. The collection includes more than 250,000 specimens and features live presentations — and even tastings (yum, tamari locusts). Visitors can also stroll through a huge open conservatory where butterflies fly free, including monarchs known for their 4,000-kilometre annual migrations across North America.

JAZZ

The Festival international de Jazz de Montréal claims to be the largest in the world: the ten-day midsummer music fest has attracted a record number of fans every year since it was formally established in 1980. Like many Montreal festivals throughout the year, the jazz fest includes free outdoor shows for audiences of all ages. The Petite école du jazz activity offers an interactive musical introduction for children. Montreal's jazz roots go back a long time: two musicians from the city's Black community, the pianist Oliver Jones and the late pianist and composer Oscar Peterson, are local virtuosos who transformed the form.

KAYAK

Kayaks are light and agile, and can move quickly on the water. Northern Indigenous people invented this watercraft about four millennia ago, using kayaks to hunt. European explorers quickly adopted it, as well as the canoe, another Indigenous invention. Kayaks originally consisted of a driftwood or whalebone frame covered with stretched seal skins and made watertight with whale fat. Today, commercially available kayaks tend to be fibreglass or plastic. Surrounded by water, the island of Montreal has some excellent kayak routes, such as the Lachine Canal, where tourists take the boats out hunting, too — for peace and quiet.

LIGHTS

Montreal is without a doubt a city of light. A rotating beacon has swept across the sky from the top of Place Ville Marie every night since 1962. Competing from the top of the mountain, the cross has shone since 1924, but the flashing beam is visible from more than 160 kilometres away. In Old Montreal, several heritage buildings, such as the Notre-Dame Basilica and city hall, are artfully lit. Among the most breathtaking light shows is the Gardens of Light event held each fall until Halloween night at the Botanical Garden, lit up with the magic of a thousand different-shaped lanterns.

MOUTHWATERING

There are so many delicious things to try in Montreal. The city loves to eat, and public markets, restaurants, bakeries, pastry shops, and food trucks offer up victuals for every palate and from every part of the world. Those with a sweet tooth might be tempted by local favourites like whippets (a Montreal invention, circa 1901) or maple sugar, or by baklava, Portuguese egg tarts, waffles, Latin American dulce de leche, gelato, panettone, cheesecake, macaroons, tartes Tatin, Black Forest cake, and Turkish delight, or by the incredible fruit of Chinatown.

NATIONS

It is thought that the earliest inhabitants of North America migrated from the Eurasian continent 12,000 years ago, and some say as early as 38,000 years. When European settlers came up the river in 1535, what is now Montreal was home to the Kanien'kehá:ka, or Mohawk, people, one group of the Haudenosaunee Confederacy. There was a fortified village, called Hochelaga. The Botanical Garden created a homage to Mohawk and other Indigenous cultures, the First Nations Garden. A Montreal neighbourhood, Hochelaga, recalls the ancestral village.

ORANGE

What's Montreal's favourite colour? Spot the clues among the clusters of pumpkins that fill market stalls in the fall, and in the spread of the trees as the leaves change. Youppi!, the current mascot of the Montreal Canadiens, is a furry fire-coloured creature. In the spring, foxes streak through some neighbourhoods. That paragon of fast food, the Gibeau Orange Julep, is located in a huge orange. And, of course, in the summer everyone gripes about the roadwork marked by endless traffic cones. Can you guess what colour?

PARADES

The beat of drums, the flash of brass bands, twirling majorettes, one incredible, original float after another... In Montreal, people take to the street for every occasion. The oldest parade is held on St. Patrick's Day: the Irish settled in Montreal in the nineteenth century, and their patron saint has been honoured annually since 1824. The St. Jean Baptiste Day parade has been going on since 1843, the Santa Claus parade since 1925, the parade to celebrate Carribean culture, Carifiesta, since 1975, and the Gay Pride parade since 1979. There's also a parade to celebrate when the Canadiens win the Stanley Cup, though the last time that happened, sadly, was way back in 1993.

QUAY

At the eastern tip of the Old Port stands the Quai de l'Horloge. The clock tower was initially built to honour sailors lost in World War I. The scene from the top is impressive: the La Ronde amusement park, the geodesic dome that houses the Biosphère science museum, the sculpture *Trois Disques (L'Homme)* by the great American artist Alexander Calder. And the St. Lawrence, which is referred to by some Indigenous people as the path that walks. Before planes, trains, and automobiles, goods and travellers came and went by boat, and Montreal came by its international economic status thanks to the river, one of the longest in the world at 3,058 kilometres. Today the Old Port welcomes in-line skaters, tourists, and anyone just out for a stroll.

RAPIDS

Upstream from the Old Port are the Lachine Rapids, a stretch of rushing current and standing waves that are a formidable natural obstacle. Over nearly five kilometres, the river drops thirteen metres, the equivalent of three storeys; the rapids are impossible for boats to cross. By the nineteenth century, the rapids could be bypassed by the then newly opened Lachine Canal. Factories popped up in this cradle of Canadian industry, which remained an important site until the 1960s, when the new St. Lawrence Seaway was created. Today, the rapids are a playground for thrill-seekers, who go rafting or even surfing there.

SANDCASTLES

Sandcastles in the middle of the river? Why not! Notre-Dame Island is an artificial island built for Expo 1967. In 1990, a small lake was opened in the island's parkland, surrounded by sand: Jean Doré Beach. The lake is fed by water from the river and filtered by aquatic plants. Historically, there have been many places to take a dip in the St. Lawrence, including at the Montreal Swimming Club, which was active between 1876 and 1950 nearby on St. Helen's Island. Some Montreal swimming holes remain, such as the bucolic beach at the Cap St. Jacques nature park in the West Island.

TOWERS

The mountain has it pretty good: a municipal bylaw prohibits construction taller than Mount Royal. The New York Life Insurance building, a stately red stone tower on Place d'Armes in Old Montreal, was the tallest building in the city when it was built in 1888, with eight floors; it even had an elevator. Other more sky-scraping constructions popped up throughout the twentieth century: in 1942, the Université de Montréal tower, with twenty-two floors, designed by Ernest Cormier; in the 1960s, the forty-two-storey Place Ville Marie, by I.M. Pei and Henry N. Cobb, was erected; and, since 1992, the highest skyscraper has stood at 1000 De La Gauchetière Street, with fifty-one floors.

UNIQUE

One of the most striking architectural features of Montreal is the exterior staircase. Sometimes spiralling up to second and third floors, Montreal's outdoor stairs are commonly found on duplex and triplex row houses built during the first half of the twentieth century. Outdoor staircases were designed to avoid wasting precious heat on indoor stairwells, and they allowed dwellings to have a private entrance. But in the winter, the ice and snow make the stairs uniquely treacherous, including for hapless mail carriers. And on the city's universal moving day of July first, having to haul a refrigerator or a piano up or down is no small task.

VIEW

For a different point of view, several top spots provide a stunning spectacle of Montreal's hundreds of steeples, its dense canopy of trees, and the city's skyline. The giant Ferris wheel in Old Montreal is a great vantage for those who aren't scared of heights. Otherwise, an elevator soars to the top of the Olympic Stadium, the tallest leaning tower in the world at 165 metres, designed by the French architect Roger Taillibert. But the most beautiful view, and the most familiar, is probably from Mount Royal's Kondiaronk Lookout, named after the Wendat chief whose diplomatic skill and eloquence helped broker the 1701 Great Peace of Montreal between New France and Indigenous peoples.

WONDER

The echoing corridors of the metro set the stage for all kinds of musicians — rock, folk, jazz, classical. The notion of promoting the arts in the urban transit system was foundational, and culture has been a part of the Montreal metro since it opened in 1966. Public artworks have been integrated into each station. The first of these commissioned pieces, at Place-des-Arts station, was created by the great artist and animated-film director Frédéric Back: *Histoire de la musique à Montréal* is a series of backlit stained glass panels. Among hundreds of cultural events, there is the Art souterrain contemporary art festival that has taken place each winter since 2009 in the tunnels that cross the downtown.

XOX

Maybe it's to warm up in the winter, or to express our Latin side: Montrealers are quite demonstrative. In the street or on public benches, Montrealers hold hands, friends clasp each other's shoulders, and couples share a smooch. La Fontaine Park, with its skating rink, ancient trees, winding paths, and cooing pigeons, is one of the most romantic parks in the city. There's another reminder of romance, too: from the top of the Musée d'art contemporain, Geneviève Cadieux's *La Voie lactée*, a giant photo of a woman's lips, blows us a kiss. From Montreal with love.

YAY!

The mountain, as Mount Royal is known to Montrealers, is a huge hill-shaped park. Some say it used to be a volcano. In 1874, Frederick Law Olmsted, an American landscape architect who also designed New York's Central Park, was entrusted with the development of a park in the heart of the city. Mount Royal is a balm in every season: there are cross-country ski trails, paths for hiking and for biking, a skating pond, white-knuckle toboggan runs, grassy slopes for luxurious sunbathing, and plenty of material for squirrel-photo safaris. On summer Sundays, Montrealers gather under the angel for the countercultural tam-tams drum jams.

ZZZ...

Even in a city that never sleeps, a nap can be nice... and sometimes necessary. Among the laziest denizens of Montreal are the two-toed sloths at the Biodôme. Everyone needs a rest, a chance to dream of the urban jungle: there's so much to see and do in Montreal.

Originally published as ABC MTL, copyright © 2017,
Jeanne Painchaud, Bruno Ricca and Éditions Les 400 Coups,
Montreal, Quebec, Canada.
Translation © Katia Grubisic, 2019.

ISBN: 978-1-77390-035-3

Linda Leith Publishing wishes to thank the Canada Council
for the Arts, the Canada Book Fund, and SODEC for their
support for our publishing program.

Photographs: Bruno Ricca, with the following exceptions:
Claude Lafond, Espace pour la vie, and Kayak, photo credit:
Julien Granger, Défi Go Fetch.
Original idea, text and haiku: Jeanne Painchaud.
Graphic design: Bruno Ricca.
Permissions: Leila Marshy.
Printed in Canada.

Linda Leith Publishing
Montreal, Canada

Library and Archives Canada Cataloguing in Publication
Title: ABC MTL / Jeanne Painchaud, Bruno Ricca ; translated
by Katia Grubisic.
Other titles: ABC MTL. English | ABCMTL | ABC Montreal
Names: Painchaud, Jeanne, author. | Ricca, Bruno,
photographer. | Grubisic, Katia, translator.
Description: Translation of: ABC MTL.
Identifiers: Canadiana (print) 20190208295 | Canadiana
(ebook) 20190208325 | ISBN 9781773900353
   (hardcover) | ISBN 9781773900360 (PDF)
Subjects: LCSH: Alphabet books—Juvenile literature. | LCSH:
English language—Alphabet—Juvenile
   literature. | LCSH: Montréal (Québec)—
   Pictorial works—Juvenile literature.
Classification: LCC PE1155 .P3513 2019 | DDC j421/.1—dc23

Panorama: View of Montreal from Habitat 67

[A] Sir George-Étienne Cartier monument, designed by George William Hill, Joseph Brunet, and Edward and William S. Maxwell

Angel atop the Notre-Dame-de-Bon-Secours Chapel

[B] St-Viateur Bagel on St. Viateur West

[D] Gorgosaurus libratus, Redpath Museum, McGill University

[F] La Joute (The Joust), Jean-Paul Riopelle, in front of the Palais des congrès convention centre

Fountain in Square St. Louis

Fountain at Place des Festivals

[H] Statue of Guy Lafleur, Place des Canadiens

Mural inspired by Serge Lemoyne's portrait Dryden in the alley near St. Lawrence north of Laurier Avenue

[K] Starting line at the Go Fetch Challenge on the St. Lawrence River

[L] The La Presse building

The exclusive Club 357c

[M] The "Guaranteed Pure Milk" water tower, 1025 Lucien-L'Allier

[N] First Nations Garden, Botanical Garden

[O] Clock Tower, Old Port of Montreal

[R] Le Monstre rollercoaster at the La Ronde amusement park

[T] Hydro-Québec building, René-Lévesque Boulevard West

St. George's Anglican Church

Place Ville Marie

1000 De La Gauchetière Street

Espace fractal (Fractal space, 2005), Jean-Pierre Morin, in front of the Grande Bibliothèque

[V] The 2-22 building, corner of St. Lawrence and St. Catherine streets

The Éperon building at the Pointe-à-Callière museum, designed by Dan S. Hanganu

Habitat 67, designed by Moshe Safdie

Jacques-Cartier bridge, designed by Philip Louis Pratley

Radio-Canada building

Montreal Olympic Stadium, designed by Roger Taillibert

Saputo Stadium

View from Kondiaronk Lookout, Mount Royal

Notre-Dame-de-Bon-Secours Chapel

Place Ville Marie

Minoterie ADM flour mill

St. Joseph's Oratory

Université de Montréal

[W] Histoire de la musique à Montréal (History of Music in Montreal, stained glass 1967), Frédéric Back, Place-des-Arts metro station

[X] The Heart of Auschwitz, Montreal Holocaust Museum, permanent exhibit

La Voie lactée (The Milky Way, 1992), Geneviève Cadieux, collection of the Musée d'art contemporain de Montréal

Aurores montréales (Aurora montrealis, (2016), Marc Séguin, projections on Mount Royal

[Y] Aurores montréales, (2016), M. Séguin

Sir George-Étienne Cartier monument, G.W. Hill, J. Brunet, E. and W.S. Maxwell

[ ] Sloth, Biodôme, photo credit Claude Lafond, Space for Life / Espace pour la vie

Panorama: View of Montreal from Kondiaronk Lookout

V for VIEW: This two-page spread consists of photos that point to other photos: one shows a location, and the dart indicates the view from that spot.

ABC... St. Cath

[ ] Les boules roses (Pink Balls, 2011), Claude Cormier + Associés, gay village

[R] Jeu de mots (Play on Words) (mural, 2012), Thomas Csano, Théâtre du Nouveau Monde

[X] Révolutions (2003), Michel de Broin, Papineau metro station

We would like to thank Space for Life / Espace pour la Vie, St-Viateur Bagel, the Olympic Stadium, Hydro-Québec, the Montreal Holocaust Museum, the STM, the Redpath Museum, Place Ville Marie, the Montreal Canadiens, Bixi, and all the partners who made this abecedarian possible.

PRINTED IN THE PRESSES OF MARQUIS IMPRIMEUR **IN** 2019
ON MARQUIS OPAQUE 376 SMOOTH PURE WHITE
TEXT IN BEBAS, DIN FONT
LAYOUT MUSIC TONY JOE WHITE